FARM CROPS

LIFE ON THE FARM

Lynn M. Stone

Rourke Publishing LLC
Vero Beach, Florida 32964

www.rourkepublishing.com

PHOTO CREDITS:
All photos © Lynn M. Stone

EDITORIAL SERVICES:
Pamela Schroeder

Library of Congress Cataloging-in-Publication Data

Stone, Lynn M.
      Farm crops / Lynn M. Stone
            p. cm. — (Life on the farm)
      Includes bibliographical references
      ISBN 1-58952-092-0
      1. Food crops—Juvenile literature. [1. Food crops.] I. Title.

SB175 .S76 2001
631.5'7—dc21   2001031669

Printed in the USA

TABLE OF CONTENTS

FARM CROPS

Crops are large numbers of food plants, such as corn, soybeans, lettuce, and oranges. About one half of American farms raise only crops.

Some crops, such as corn, are planted in fields. Others are the fruits of trees or bushes. Apples, oranges, and cherries are tree crops. Fruit trees make up a grove or **orchard**.

Summer sunshine bathes a corn crop in the Midwest.

Most crop farms grow and sell crops only. They raise one or two crops most of the time. Many corn farmers, for example, also raise soybeans.

Livestock farms often raise crops to feed their animals. But livestock farmers don't often raise crops to sell.

Mmmm, good! A Jersey cow gobbles greens.

Crops are important for animals as well as people. Farmers feed food crops to livestock. Then livestock becomes food for us. Without crops there would be no hamburgers, steaks, or fried eggs!

The most important American crops are cereal **grains**. Corn is the most important cereal grain. It is one of the crops used for food by both people and farm animals. Another important cereal grain is wheat.

Corn is the most important crop grown by American farmers.

WHERE CROPS GROW

Each kind of plant has different needs. Nearly all crop plants need sunshine, soil, and water. But each crop needs the right kind of weather. Oranges, sugar cane, and bananas, for example, grow only where there is no hard frost. Apple trees, however, need a cold season.

Apples do well in many northern states.

Family farms harvest garden crops like these throughout the summer.

Montana hay bales lie drying on a September afternoon.

Different kinds of corn will grow almost anywhere. But corn is at its best in the rich, black soil of the Midwest. Wheat does well in the dry plains states.

Many parts of North America are famous for their crops. Florida and California have their oranges. Manitoba and Alberta in Canada, have their wheat. Louisiana has sugar. Washington, Michigan, and New York have their apples. Illinois and Iowa are known for their corn and soybeans.

Florida is known for its groves of juicy oranges and grapefruit.

PLANTING CROPS

Each crop grows during a special time of year called a season. Each crop has its own season. Some crops in warm states may have two or three growing seasons.

Farmers plant their field crops at the beginning of the season. Illinois corn, for example, is usually planted in late April.

Farmers make their fields ready for seeding by tilling the soil with machines.

First farmers must make their fields ready for planting. Farmers loosen the soil with plows or **discs**. They use tractors and special machines to plant seeds.

Plants need water to grow. Rainfall isn't always enough. Some farmers bring water to their fields in canals or with huge **sprayers**.

Huge sprayers send jets of water onto crops in south Florida.

HARVESTING CROPS

Farmers **harvest** at the end of the season. By then the fruits and vegetables have stopped growing. Now they are ripe and ready for picking. Oranges and apples are often picked by hand. But most crops are harvested by machines. Ears of corn and soybeans, for example, are picked by a **combine**. Different harvesting machines are built to gather other crops.

A corn combine harvests ears of Illinois corn from their stalks.

After harvest, farmers send their crops to market or store them. Some crops are ground up before being stored. Cattle farmers often crush corn crops into animal food called **silage**. Silage is stored in **silos**.

GLOSSARY

combine (KAHM byn) — a machine that harvests grain

crop (KRAHP) — a field, orchard, or grove of ripening food plants, such as corn or apples

disc (DISK) — a farm machine used to plow soil and equipped with several round blades

grain (GRAYN) — the seed or fruit of a cereal grass plant, such as corn or wheat

harvest (HAR vist) — to gather in a crop

livestock (LYV stahk) — farm animals

orchard (OR churd) — a planted group of fruit trees, especially apples, pears, and cherries

silage (SY lij) — animal food that is stored in a silo

silo (SY loh) — a tube-shaped building where animal food is stored

sprayer (SPRAY er) — a machine that sprays water

INDEX

Further Reading

Cooper, Jason. *Corn*. Rourke, 1998.

Cooper, Jason. *Oranges*. Rourke, 1998

Paladino, Catherine. *One Good Apple: Growing Our Food for the Sake of the Earth*. Houghton Mifflin, 1999

Stone, Lynn M. *Pumpkins*. Rourke, 2002.

Websites To Visit

www.historylink101.com

About The Author

Lynn Stone is the author of more than 400 children's books. He is a talented natural history photographer as well. Lynn, a former teacher, travels worldwide to photograph wildlife in its natural habitat.